Horn   Intermediate Level

MASTER SOLOS
by Louis Stout

EDITED by Linda Rutherford

Contents

To access companion recorded performances
and accompaniments online, visit:
www.halleonard.com/mylibrary

Enter Code
7077-9561-0750-5830

ISBN 978-0-7935-9552-5

HAL•LEONARD®

Visit Hal Leonard Online at
www.halleonard.com

Contact us:
Hal Leonard
7777 West Bluemound Road
Milwaukee, WI 53213
Email: info@halleonard.com

In Europe, contact:
Hal Leonard Europe Limited
42 Wigmore Street
Marylebone, London, W1U 2RN
Email: info@halleonardeurope.com

In Australia, contact:
Hal Leonard Australia Pty. Ltd.
4 Lentara Court
Cheltenham, Victoria, 3192 Australia
Email: info@halleonard.com.au

Introducing

Mr. Louis Stout

As an educator, performer, and author, Mr. Stout ranks in the forefront of horn specialists. Prior to his present appointment at the University of Michigan, he taught at the Chicago School of Music, the Kansas City Conservatory, and Ithaca College. He is still teaching at the New England Music Camp during the summer. Mr. Stout's professional background includes the Chicago Symphony, Kansas City Philharmonic, New Orleans Symphony, Radio City Music Hall, North Carolina Symphony, and the Virginia Symphony. He has published many articles and reviews for music magazines and journals and is a noted clinician/lecturer/soloist with bands and orchestras in the United States and Canada. His contribution as an educator has been widespread as seen by the number of former students who are prominently active in both the academic and professional fields.

This series of solos was specifically designed to conform with the requirements of the many Solo and Ensemble Contest Festivals. They have been chosen so that each piece will present to the adjudicator the elements of performance so necessary to a correct evaluation. The time limitation is also a consideration so the length of each has been structured in the two to four minute length.

More specifically, the material had the following objectives:

1. To present highest quality music from the Baroque, Classical, Romantic, Impressionistic and Contemporary periods.
2. To keep the difficulty of the solos within the technical limits of this particular level.
3. To select solos which could improve your artistic and technical capabilities.
4. To present in each piece some examples of the principal-categories of the grading, such as Tone Quality, Intonation, Technic, Rhythm, Articulation and Interpretation.

Mr. Louis Stout, Jr., a student at the University of Michigan, will perform each solo on the recording. He will be accompanied by Mrs. Lillian Holtfreter.

It is our hope that you will enjoy this innovative approach to music study and development. The care in preparation is of course the prime factor in a successful presentation.

HAL•LEONARD®
7777 W. BLUEMOUND RD. P.O. BOX 13819 MILWAUKEE, WI 53213

Come Unto Him

musical terms

larghetto — slow and solemn but not quite as slow as largo
a tempo — return to the tempo which preceded a variation in tempo

Handel was born in Saxony in 1685 and died in London in 1759. He was one of the most prolific composers of all times, but will be eternally famous for his Water Music Suite and Messiah, performed during the Christmas and Easter seasons. Beethoven said of Handel, "He is the greatest, ablest composer that ever lived." He traveled extensively throughout his life, and this contributed greatly to the international flavor of his compositions.

This solo is a soprano solo from the Messiah. It is not a fast solo, but is marked by a lovely, legato style of playing. This requires good breath control. Practice taking deep, full breaths, feeling all parts of your chest and back expand to their fullest. Your air should be blown out slowly and gradually, so that you are able to play long phrases easily. Breath support can be compared with taking a full breath and then blowing up a balloon. This resistance of the balloon is similar to the resistance of the horn. It is that resistance against which you push your air column. This should all be done in a natural, relaxed·manner for the most lovely tone production.

Be careful to observe all of the slurs in this solo, and all notes that are tongued should be done with a very gentle tongue, using the syllable "Doo." A singer would use vibrato in singing this solo, but the vibrato is not characteristic of the horn. Try to play with a steady, level tone quality. The beauty of the horn tone is in its intensity and pure quality.

In each of the solos in this book, you will find markings such as M.M. ♩=100. M.M. stands for Maelzel's Metronome, the inventor of the metronome. This particular marking means that the metronome should be set at 100, and each click of the metronome will represent the length or speed of one quarter note.

The metronome marking for the solo, "Come Unto Him," is M.M. ♪=132. This solo is written in 12/8 time, meaning there are 12 eighth notes per measure, and each of them will get one beat of the metronome, which you will have set at 132. If at first you are unable to play the solo at the given marking, you should feel free to set the metronome marking to a smaller number and gradually work the solo up the suggested setting.

Various combinations of eighth notes used in this solo are ♪=1 beat ♩=2 beats ♩.=3 beats ♩.=6 beats.

Measures 1-6 You and your accompanist begin together. You should get the tempo set in your mind and then give a small downbeat with your horn, so that you can both play the eighth note pick-up together.

3

Start the solo softly with a good clear tone. In measure 2
there is a new rhythm of a dotted eighth-sixteenth. Think of
the dotted eighth as three tied sixteenths ahead of the single
sixteenth note. Practice the following exercise to become
familiar with 12/8 time and the different rhythm
patterns used.

PREPARATION 1

Measures 7-14 These measures are an exact repeat of the
first six measures. You should play them in the same way.
Since this solo is an arrangement of a voice solo, you should
strive to play as smoothly and legato as the human voice.
Measure 12 is the piano alone which introduces the same
melody that the horn plays in measure 13.

Measures 15-19   Measure 15 starts an upward moving
passage that should push forward, giving a measure of
excitement to the passage. The accompaniment also has
this crescendo. After this crescendo, there is a descending
passage that gets softer and slightly slower.

Measures 20-31   This is an exact repetition of measures
12-19. As you finish your solo diminuendo a bit more. The
piano completes the solo.

Come Unto Him

George Frederic Handel
(1685 - 1759)

A Tear

musical terms

andante con moto — slowly with motion
cantabile — in a singing style
largo — slowly and solemnly

Modest Moussorgsky was born in Karevo, Russia, in 1839, and died in St. Petersburg in 1881. He simply tried to translate into sound the soul's cries, which struck upon his ears from without or rose from within himself. This horn solo represents just one of the many torments of his life that he translated into music.

Usually a "tear" comes at a sad or lonely time of life. This solo is written in a minor key, which is often called the "sad" key. The difference between a major and a minor key is the difference in the combination of whole and half steps. The illustration below shows the D major scale and three forms of a d minor scale. All three forms are often used within one solo.

ILLUSTRATION 1

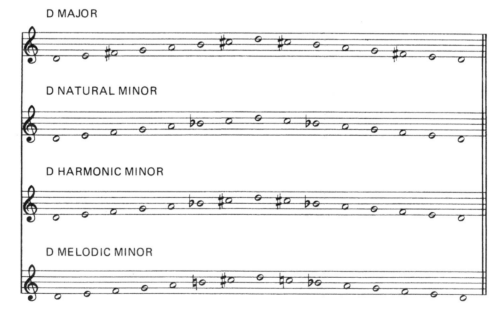

Even Moussorgsky tried to fight his way up from the depths of this unhappiness, as shown by the section of the solo in D major. But this is short-lived and the music returns to d minor and ends in a very quiet and moody way.

To become familiar with the minor tonality practice the
following exercise.

PREPARATION 2

Measures 1-12 This solo starts with a soft, singing style,
not too fast, even though the marking is "Andante con
moto". Since this section is in the minor key, you do want
to set up a certain mood. You will need a certain amount of
motion in order to be able to play three-measure phrases in
one breath. Support well to get nice smooth slurs in measure
12 and ritard slightly to close the "sad" section.

Measures 13-23 This measure starts the happier, more
optimistic section of the music. It starts softly and never gets
too loud. With a definitely faster tempo and the change to
the key of D major, you can give an impression of momen-
tary hopefulness and joy. However, all of this happiness is
short-lived and the feeling of despair returns.

Measures 24-36 The key of d minor and the slower
tempo return. It is always a challenge to see of you are able
to establish the same tempo as the beginning. The music is
like the beginning section. Once again, support the upward
slurs in measure 32.

In measure 33 begin slowing down for the last four measures.
Be sure you get a good breath so you can fade out the last
notes to almost nothing. This is a beautiful effect and one
that the horn can do so very well in this particular register.

A Tear

Modest Moussorgsky
(1839-1881)

Träumerei

musical terms

andante — in moderate time, but flowing easily and gracefully
dim. (diminuendo) — means decrescendo, a word denoting a decreasing power of tone

new note

F

F Horn

B♭ Horn
Double Horn - add thumb key

Robert Schumann was born in 1810 in Saxony. He began piano lessons when he was six years old. His early musical life was greatly influenced by the songs of Schubert. After his father died, he was forced by his strong-willed mother to pursue a career in law. He was not happy doing so and gradually devoted his full time to piano study. However, due to an unfortunate mechanical device that he used to hopefully develop flexibility in his fingers, he soon developed paralysis in both of the fingers he had hoped to help. His virtuoso career now ended, he had to turn to full time composition of music.

His compositions include much piano music, many songs, four symphonies, and chamber music. One of his piano pieces was <u>Kinderscenen</u> (<u>Scenes from Childhood</u>), composed in 1838. There are 13 parts of this work, each descriptive of childhood memories. "Träumerei" ("Dreaming") is one of these scenes and is a mood picture.

The range of this solo is one step short of two octaves, which is probably more than you are accustomed to. Practice the following exercise to help develop your range.

PREPARATION 3

You will also need good lip slurs in this solo. Lip slurs are the result of connecting two or more notes together smoothly, without tonguing. An upward slur is done by tightening the lips together to produce the higher vibration necessary for the higher note. This is also accompanied by the arching of the tongue towards the roof of the mouth, as if going from the syllable "ah" to "ee". Work on the following exercises to develop smooth slurs. Be sure to keep good firm breath support behind these slurs, otherwise they will tend to "stick".

PREPARATION 4

PREPARATION 5

Measures 1-8 You have the pick-up at the beginning so your accompanist will listen to you for the tempo. In measure 8 there is a new musical notation called a grace note. This is a note that decorates or embellishes the note on the beat. Since this solo is slower and more relaxed, the grace note is not played too quickly. Practice the following exercise to become familiar with grace notes.

PREPARATION 6

AHEAD OF THE BEAT | | ON THE BEAT

Measures 9-17 Get a good breath before measure 13, for this is where you approach the new note, high "F". It is also the loudest volume of this solo. In measures 15 and 16 you diminuendo in volume and ritard slightly. It should slow down enough so that you are able to make a small pause before the low "G" pick-up in measure 17.

The dotted eighth-sixteenth pattern in measure 16 is new to you. Think of the dotted eighth note as three tied sixteenth notes. The following exercise will help you prepare for this new rhythm.

PREPARATION 7

Measures 18-24 In measure 22 you have a fermata or hold. There is no exact amount of time given to a fermata, it is usually left up to the individual performer. You have the three pick-up notes to measure 23, so it will be easy for your accompanist to know when to join you. The whole ending section should be taken very slowly with as much ritard as you can control and with a diminuendo to a very soft and quiet ending. It will help if you take another breath before the last three notes. Then you can easily hold the last note to a very soft conclusion.

Träumerei

Robert Schumann
(1810-1856)

(M.M. ♩=54)
Andante

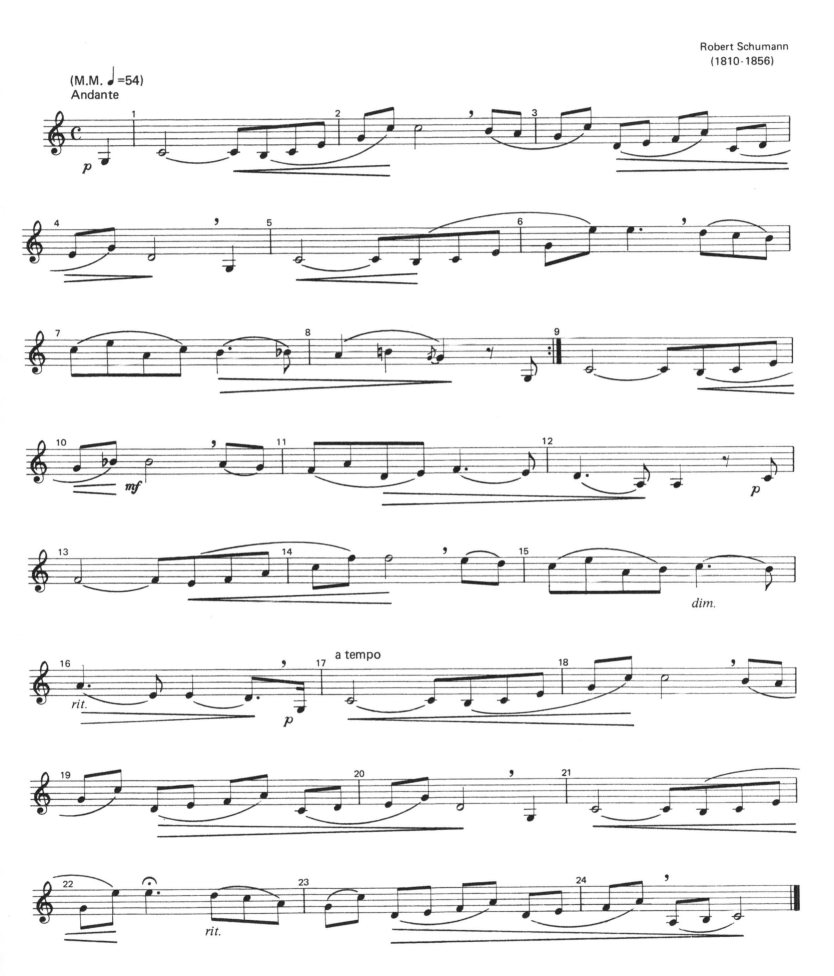

The Swan

musical terms

adagio e tranquillo — slowly and peacefully
piu mosso — more motion
lento — slowly

Camille Saint-Saens was born in Paris in 1835 and died in Algiers in 1921. He started piano lessons at the age of 2½ and by five was composing piano pieces and songs. He was respected as the finest composer of France. "The Swan" is one movement of a suite for two pianos and orchestra entitled Le Carnaval des Animaux (The Carnival of the Animals). This is the most celebrated movement of the entire suite. A beautiful, serene melody for the cello simulates the majestic movements of the swan. This melody has been arranged for horn for this book.

This solo is written with a meter signature of 6/4, meaning that there are six beats in a measure and a quarter note will get one beat. Likewise, other note values are similar to those you have already seen in 4/4 time. ♩ gets two beats, ♩. gets three beats, o gets four beats, o. gets six beats. Practice the following exercises to become familiar with this meter signature.

PREPARATION 8

PREPARATION 9

All the phrases in this piece are two measures long, however, with each measure receiving six beats, it will be necessary to exercise good breath control. Blow your air out slowly with good muscle support from the diaphragm. You will also notice that all of the tongued notes have a long dash over or under the notes. Remember that this denotes legato tonguing. You should pronounce the syllable "Doo" as you tongue, trying to make the notes as connected as possible.

Measures 1-8 In measures 2 and 6, do not underestimate the difficulty of the downward slurs of a fifth. Be sure to keep good breath support, keep the wind moving, or you may get a break in the tone that you do not wish. In measures 4 and 7 you have the legato tonguing on the upward progressing runs. Set the diaphragm support for the highest note at the bottom note of the run, then you will go upward with ease and freedom. One of the most important things in this solo is a very smooth slur, to denote the very smooth and effortless way that a swan moves across the water.

Measures 9-13 Measure 9 is the loudest part of this solo. Try to work up to a very exciting sound. Measure 10 starts at the same level, but then gradually diminishes as you return to the lower register. Measure 12 begins in the same way. This is a most lovely effect you can hear on the tape.

Measures 14-17 Measures 14 and 15 are a very effective crescendo through the first measure and a decrescendo through the second measure. Measures 16 and 17 are a repeat of this effect, but measure 17 has a ritard. The horn part is very easy here, but you must listen carefully to the piano part to know just when to move to your fourth beat of the measure. The piano has four notes to each beat and they are quite easy to hear.

Measures 18-21 Measures 18-21 are a repeat of the beginning phrase. Remember to keep up the breath support on the downward slurs of a fifth. Measure 22 is again one of the louder parts of the piece and starts a gradual diminuendo to the very end. Observe the lento in measure 25. These three notes are slower than you have been playing. Measure 26 begins the "a tempo". Get a big breath here so you can hold out the last note full length. Also try to diminuendo this note to nothing.

The Swan

Camille Saint-Saens
(1835-1921)

MASTER SOLOS INTERMEDIATE LEVEL

Edited by Louis Stout, Sr.
Performed by Louis Stout, Jr.

Horn

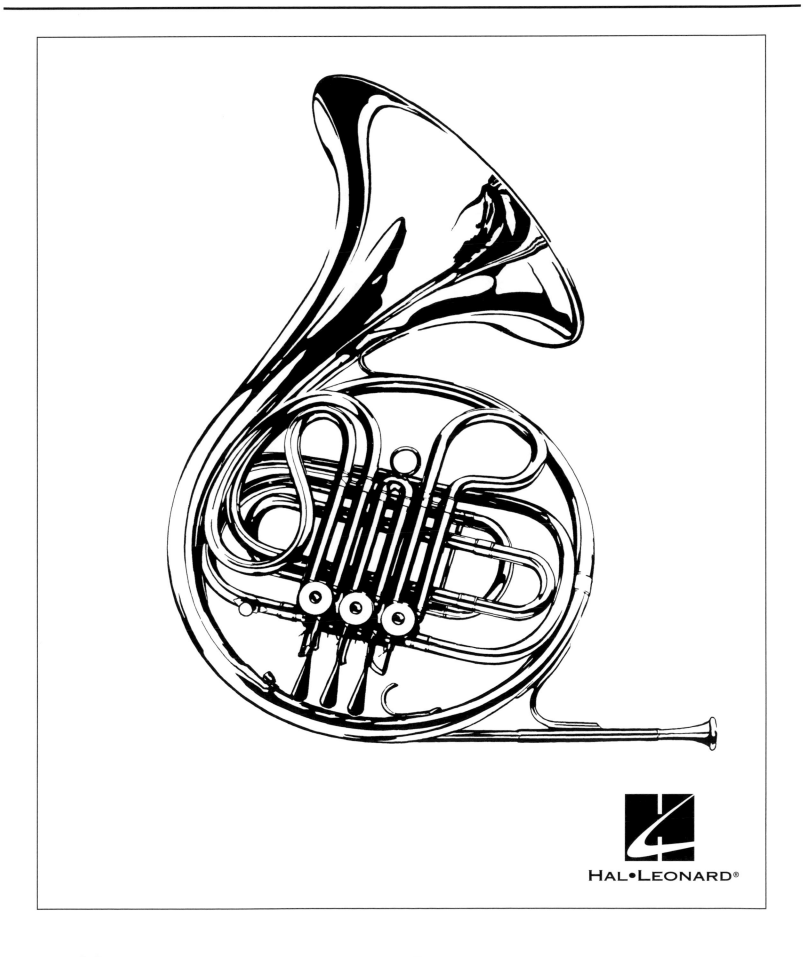

HAL•LEONARD®

Come Unto Him

George Frederic Handel
(1685-1759)

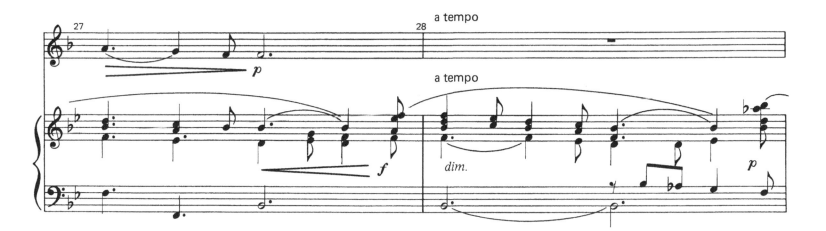

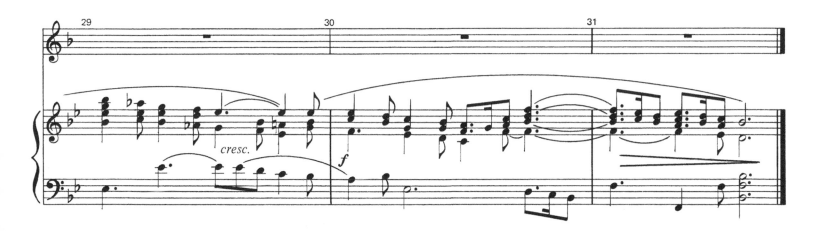

A Tear

Modest Moussorgsky
(1839-1881)

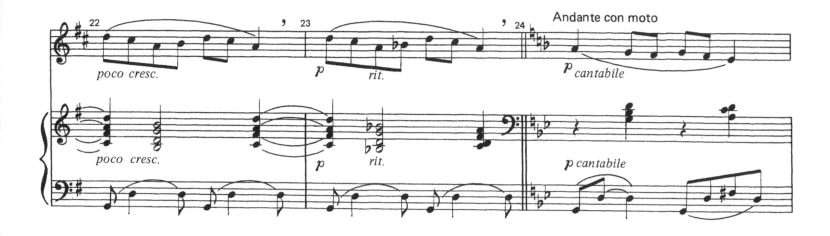

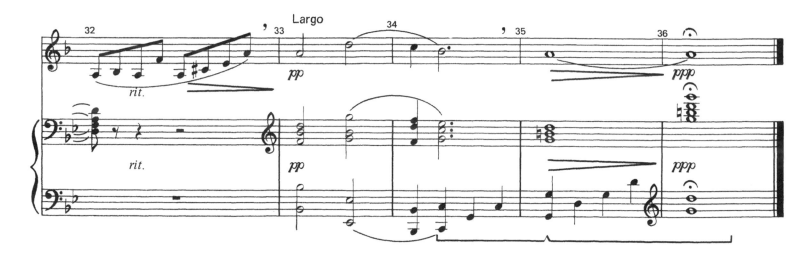

Träumerei

Robert Schumann
(1810-1856)

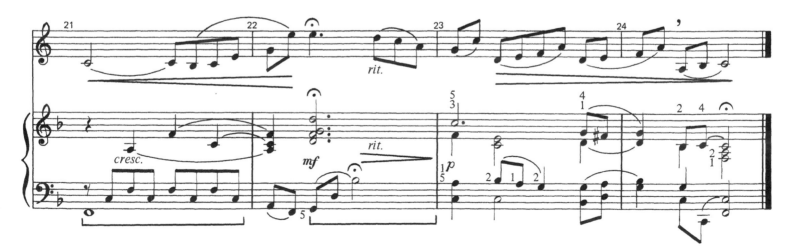

The Swan

Camille Saint-Saens
(1835-1921)

(M.M. ♩=68)
Adagio e Tranquillo

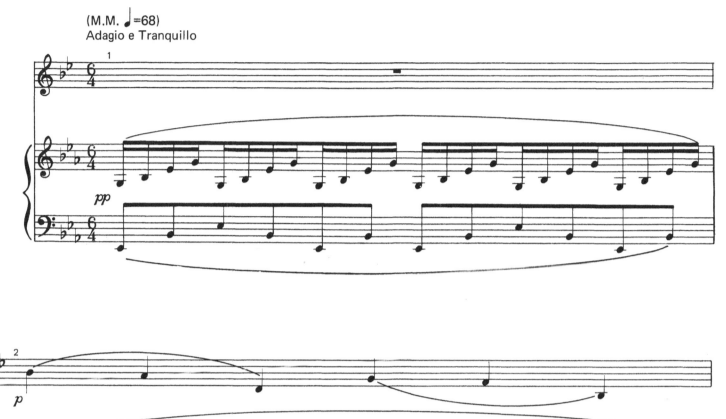

11

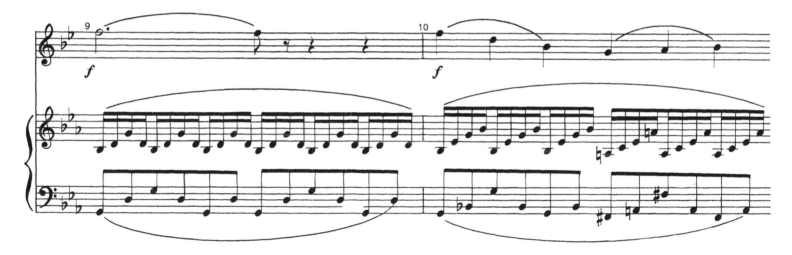

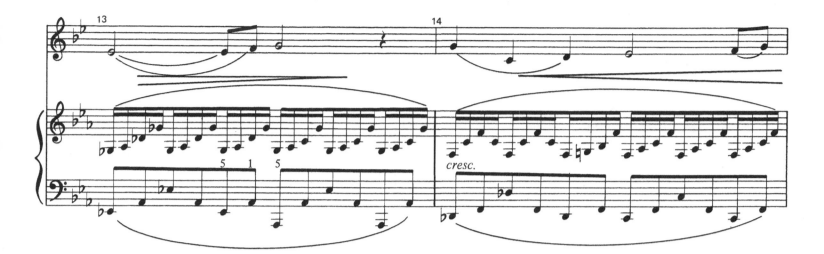

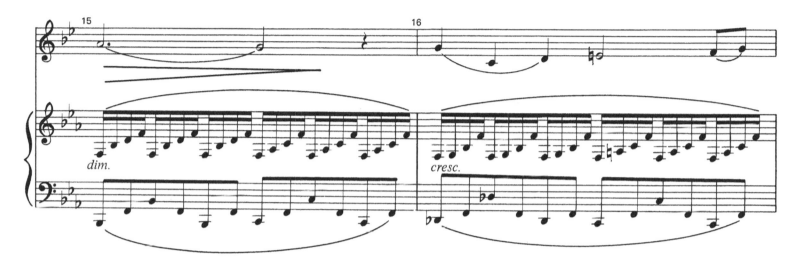

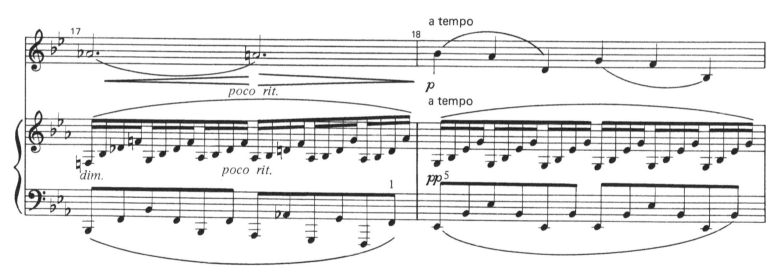

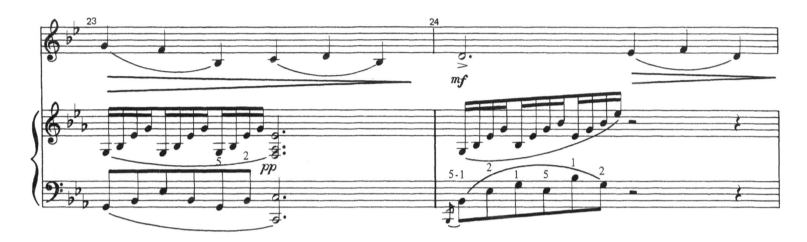

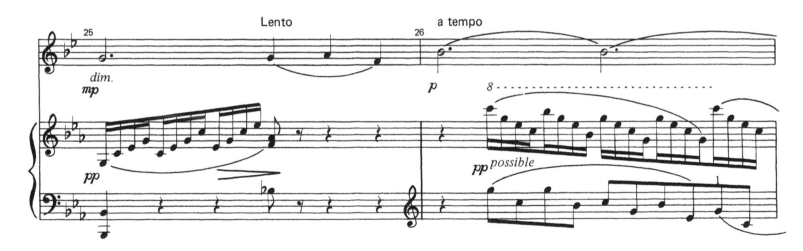

14

Sicilienne

Giovanni Pergolesi
(1710-1736)

16

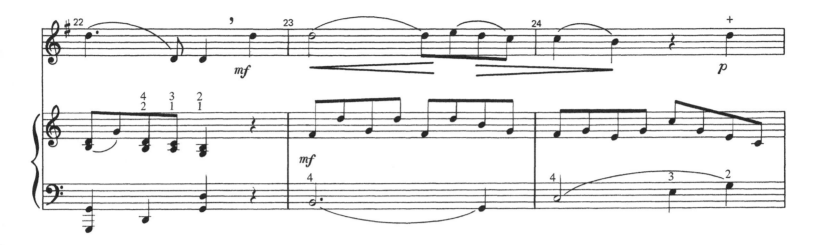

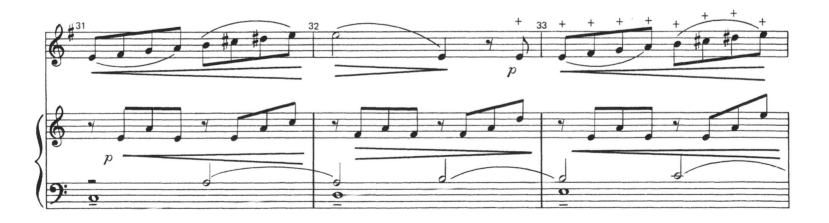

17

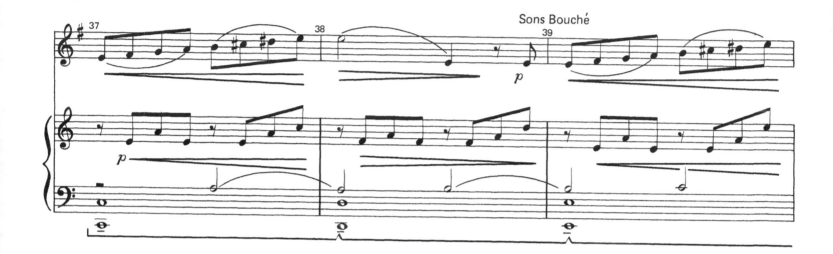

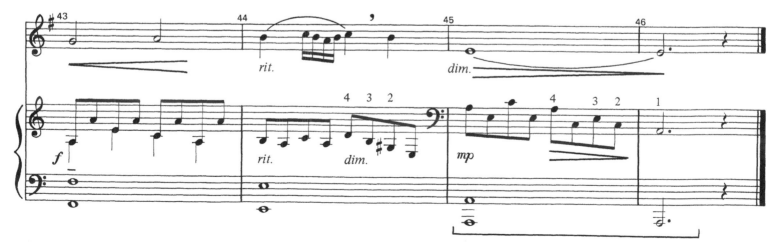

Romance

Camille Saint-Saens
(1835-1921)

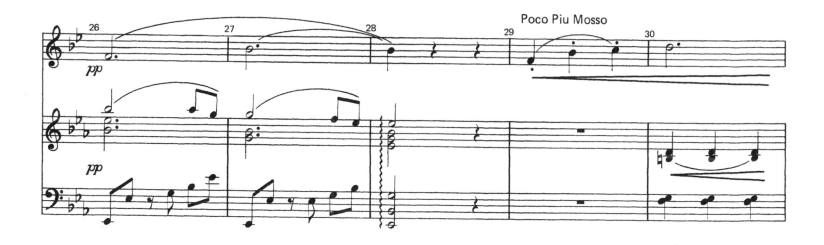

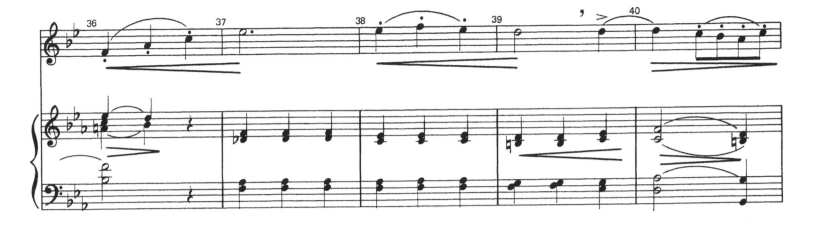

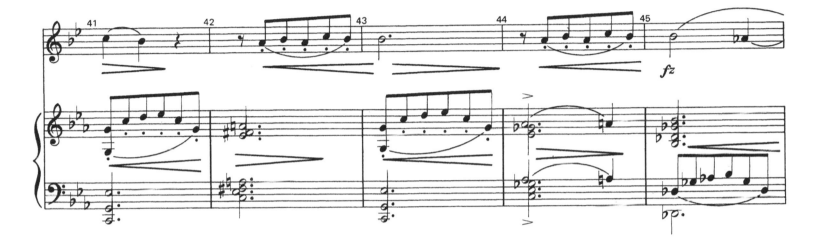

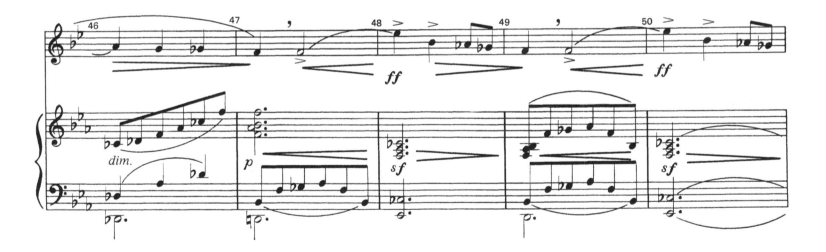

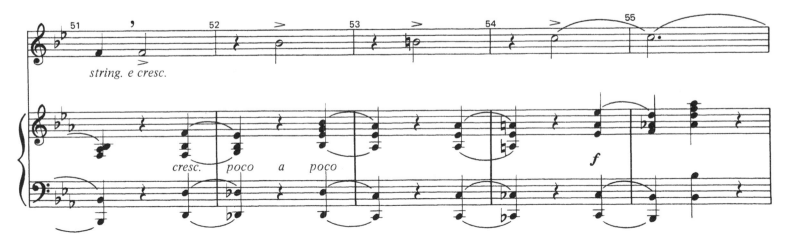

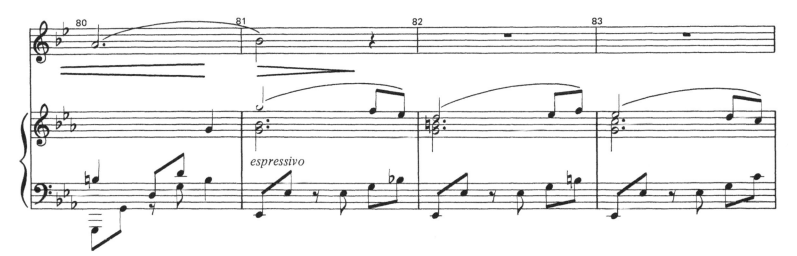

Air

Johann Sebastian Bach
(1685-1750)

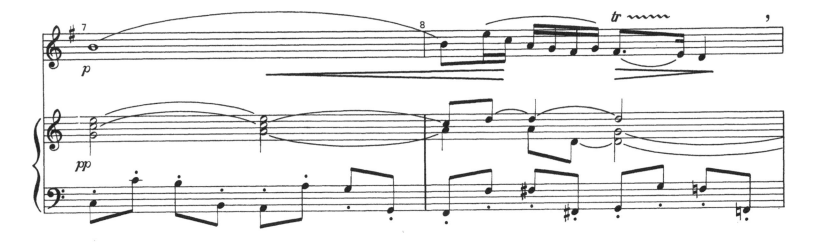

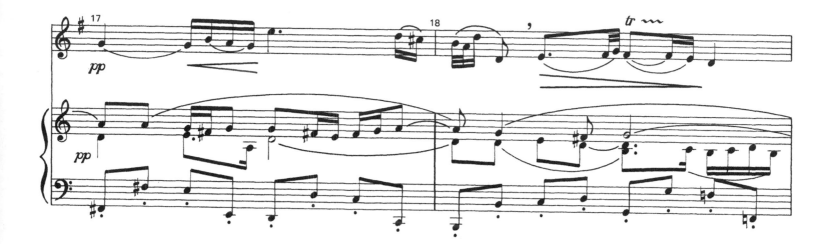

Movement For Horn And Piano

Gordon Stout

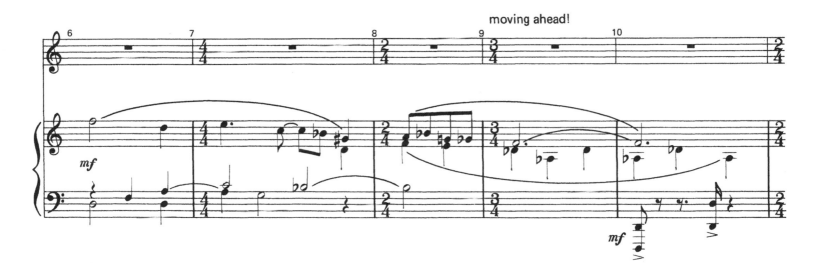

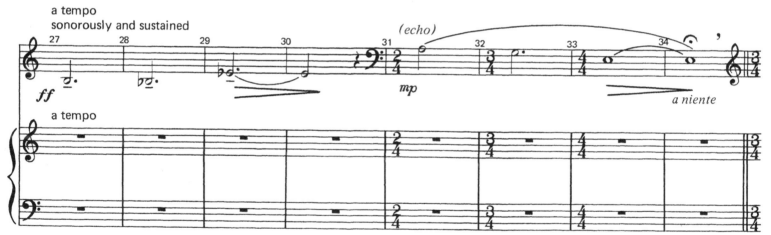

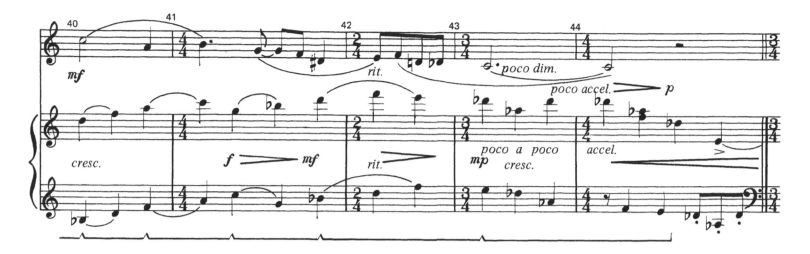

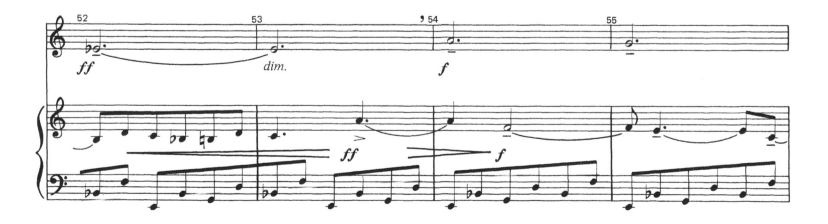

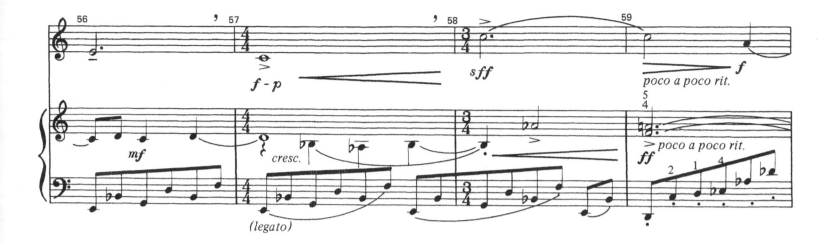

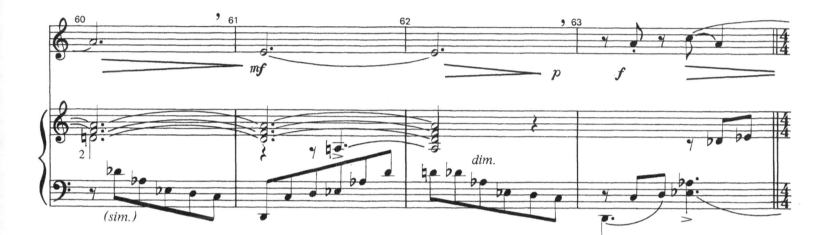

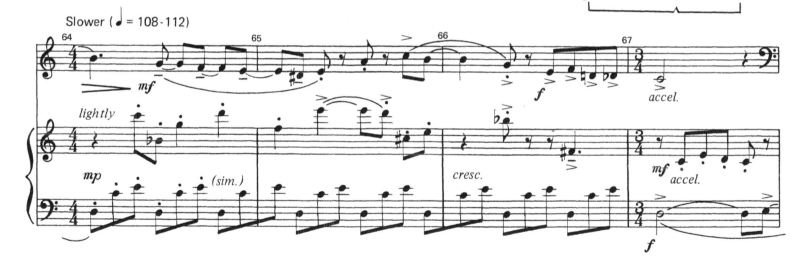

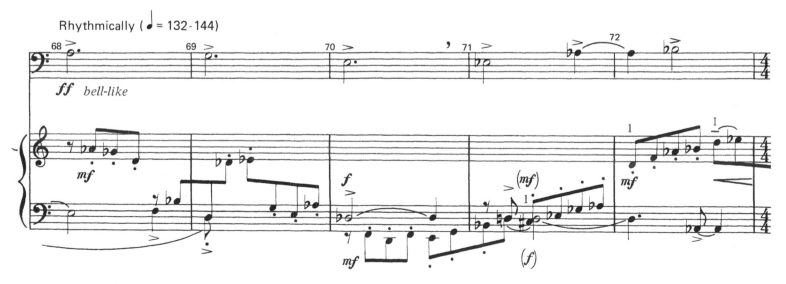

Broadly and Slower (♩=112)

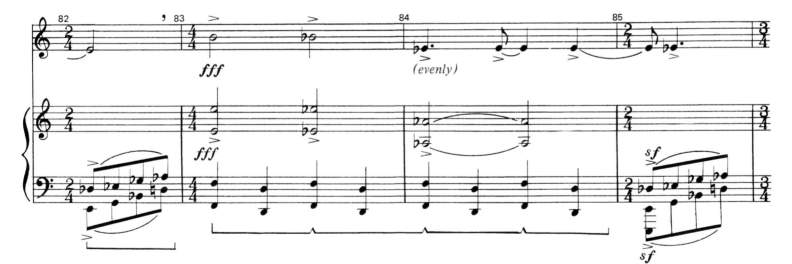

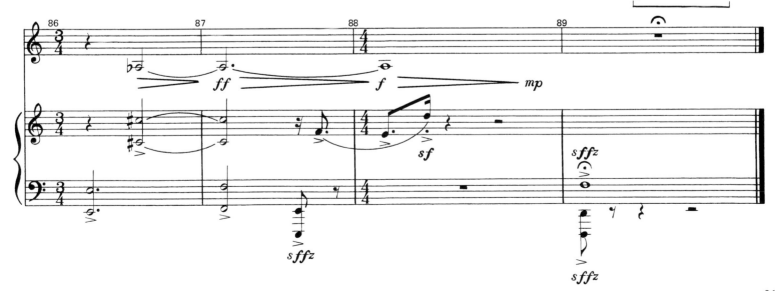

Sicilienne

musical terms

andantino — a little slower than andante; flowing easily along
sons bouche — stopped sound, produced by putting the right hand tightly in the bell of the horn
sons ouvert — opening the right hand up again to produce normal tones
+ — sign above notes that indicates they are stopped

new note

G

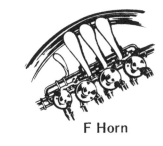

F Horn

Bb Horn
Double Horn - add thumb key

Giovanni Pergolesi was one of the early leaders of the Baroque period. He was born in Italy in 1710 and died in 1736. His contributions to comic opera and the sonata form were later carried on by many other composers.

This solo has much more of the legato tonguing, so you must now begin to realize that this is one of the most important kinds of tonguing that you can learn. Below is an exercise to help you develop your legato tonguing.

A "sicilienne" is a form of peasant dance that was used frequently in Baroque instrumental music. It is usually written in a moderately slow tempo.

PREPARATION 10

Measures 1-12 Listen carefully to the piano introduction, so that you are ready to make your entrance. In measures 5-7 you have some very effective crescendos and decrescendos that add much to the expression of the piece.

Measure 10 has a triplet that is played on the second half of the beat (the 2nd eighth note of beat 1). A triplet is a rhythmic figure which divides a note into three equal parts. In this measure, the eighth note is divided into three equal parts (three sixteenth notes). Practice the following exercise to help you develop this embellishment.

PREPARATION 11

In measure 11 there is another triplet, this one is an eighth note triplet on one beat. The following exercise will help you prepare for this figure in the solo.

Measures 13-20   This is a repetition of the first twelve measures. Continue to play the tenuto notes with legato tonguing.

Measures 21-26   Measure 24 is the beginning of the stopped passages. Probably most of you are familiar with using a mute to produce a softer tone or a different tone color on the horn. Hand stopping is another of the interesting tonal effects that can be produced on the horn. It is done by closing the right hand tightly in the bell of the horn. Your hand should be at right angles across the bell as much

as possible. Do not merely shove your hand as far down the throat of the bell as you can. This will put your hand too far into the horn and will make a very sharp pitch, especially those of you with smaller hands. Bring the hand back as far as you can and still effectively close the bell, trying to get your hand at right angles across the bell. Think of placing a round disc across the bell of the horn. When you get your hand correctly placed, you will notice that the pitch of the notes will raise by one **half-step**. You will have to finger any stopped notes one **half-step** lower to produce the correct pitch. The illustration below shows one of the stopped passages with the correct fingerings for an F horn.

ILLUSTRATION 2

This note open

This hand stopping and the resulting pitch can only happen on a single F horn or the F side of a double horn. If you have a B♭ horn, you must have a stopping valve on the horn in order to stop this passage. If you have the stopping valve, depress the valve, stop your hand in the bell, and play the notes just as they are written. It will **not** be necessary for you to transpose the notes one **half-step** lower. If you have a B♭ horn without a stopping valve, you will have to try to very quickly insert a mute into the bell of the horn for these passages. This can be accomplished by attaching a circle of

string to the end of your mute and hanging the mute around your wrist where you can get it very quickly, when needed.

Measures 27-40   Measure 33 starts the most lengthy of the stopped passages. It is marked with the words "sons bouche", which means to stop all notes until you come to the words "sons ouvert", at which time you will again open the bell of the horn. Below is that passage with the fingerings for the single F horn.

ILLUSTRATION 3

The important thing to remember when playing the stopped passages, is that they should be in tune. At first, you should play those passages open to get the sound "fixed" in your mind. Later play them stopped, listening carefully to the tuning. In this piece, you are fortunate that the stopped passages are exact repetitions of the same notes that you have already played open. This will make it easier for you to tune the passages.

Measures 41-46   Measure 41 has a ritard, be careful not to rush. Three measures from the end is a sixteenth note turn. Take your time, for you are setting up the mood for the final measures. Try to let your tone fade to nothing.

Sicilienne

Giovanni Pergolesi
(1710-1736)

Romance

musical terms

moderato — moderate tempo
poco piu mosso — a little more motion
stringendo — accelerating the tempo
tempo I — return to the original tempo
a piacere — at your pleasure

Camille Saint-Saens was born in Paris in 1835 and died in Algiers in 1921. Although Saint-Saens was a prolific composer (over 200 compositions), much of his work has not survived except for his orchestral works. "Romance" was originally written for horn and orchestra. In this version, the orchestra parts have been arranged into the piano accompaniment.

Every aspect of playing improves with good breath control: tone quality, intonation, range, endurance, articulation, and lip slurs. This is the source of all success. Remember to

take full, relaxed breaths, then exert muscular pressure with your diaphragm muscles to put the air under pressure. In this way you are able to get better results with a smaller quantity of air. This is known as breath control, making the very best possible use of the air.

Measures 1-20 The articulation used in measure 3 and throughout the solo is a dot under a slur. This denotes legato tonguing again and is achieved by using the syllable "Doo" as you tongue. Be sure to use lots of breath support so that your legato tonguing will not be inclined to "stick". Practice this legato tonguing in the following exercise.

PREPARATION 13

In measure 13 start to crescendo to the "E♭" in measure 15. Measure 15 is a beautiful area and the forte level gives you an opportunity to play a very nice diminuendo from measure 16 through measure 18.

Measures 21-41   Another four-measure crescendo begins in measure 21 and moves to measure 24. Be careful not to diminuendo too quickly in measures 24, 25, and 26 or you may find the lip slur to "B♭" in measure 27 difficult to play.

The section starting at measure 29 is a little faster. The accent in measures 32 and 39 is an important effect in the phrase. This entire section has a feeling of movement, restlessness, and anxiety.

Measures 42-65   Measure 42 continues this surging feeling leading through two repeated measures to the heavy accent at measure 45, with just a bit of decrescendo to measure 47. However, the biggest and fastest crescendo to the loudest dynamic of the entire piece comes at measures 48 and 50. This is the emotional climax of the whole piece.

Measure 51 starts a five-measure section that gets even faster (stringendo). Observe the accented notes on the second beats of these five measures. At measure 56, there is a fast diminuendo to a "pp" in measures 58 and 59. A relaxation in tempo is also in order here. Listen carefully to the tape to see just how much is done. The mood continues to relax to the fermata in measure 65.

Measures 66-93   Measure 66 is once again the tempo of the beginning of the piece. You will also notice a return to the more gentle legato tonguing. Build to a climactic volume at measure 78.

Measure 84 starts what might be called a coda or ending. It is new music that continues to get softer and softer from measure 85 to the end. Once again, do not start your diminuendo too fast or too soon, or you may find it difficult to continue it to the end. You do not want to "lose" your last note, but do try to fade this piece to nothing.

Romance

Camille Saint-Saens
(1835-1921)

Air

musical term

poco a poco — little by little

new note

F♯

F Horn

B♭ Horn
Double Horn - add thumb key

Johann Sebastian Bach was born in Eisenach in 1685 and died in Leipzig in 1750. He was one of the most prolific composers of all time, although most of his music was not published until 75 years after his death. Because of this, during his lifetime he was not considered as great as other members of the great Bach family. But today, his compositional excellence is considered the height of the Baroque era. Richard Wagner called him the "most stupendous miracle in all of music". The "Air" was originally composed for violin and is known today as the famous Air for the G String. It is adapted here for the horn with piano accompaniment.

The new challenge of this solo is the fact that it is written in 4/4 time, but it is actually played with eight beats to the measure. An eighth note will receive one beat. The whole note of the first measure receives a full eight beats and ties over for another two beats of the second measure. Two sixteenth notes will receive one beat, and four thirty-second notes will receive one beat. Watch the note values carefully as you listen to the tape, then practice the following exercises to help you get used to the note values for this solo.

but most of the crescendo will take place on the moving notes. This is a general rule of music: Bring out the moving notes.

Measures 1-12 Measure 1 should have a gradual crescendo to a peak at the beginning of measure 2, followed by a nice diminuendo. In measure 3 the held note has a small crescendo,

In measure 2 there is a new rhythmic figure, a trill. A trill is the rapid alternation of the written pitch and the note above it. The illustration below shows how it is written and how it should be played. This trill is easily fingered and should present no problems.

ILLUSTRATION 4

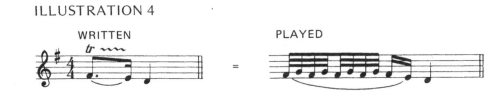

Measures 13-24   Be careful of the note values all the way through this solo. Remember that each phrase starts softly, crescendos quite a bit, and fades back again at the end of the phrase. The trill in measure 18 should be played like the trill in measure 2.

You will most likely need the extra breath to handle the crescendo in measures 19 and 20. The loudest climactic point in this solo is in measure 22. Measure 23 starts a very gradual diminuendo to the end.

The trill in measure 24 should be played as shown.

ILLUSTRATION 5

Take lots of time for the ritard in measure 24 and don't rush the trill.

Air

Johann Sebastian Bach
(1685-1750)

Movement For Horn And Piano

musical terms

molto — much or very much
a niente — to nothing; diminish to nothing
espressivo — expressively, with feeling
accel. (accelerando) — get faster
sostenuto — sustained, smoothly

new notes

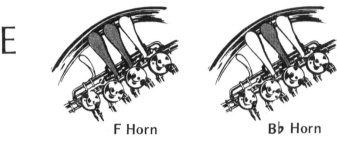

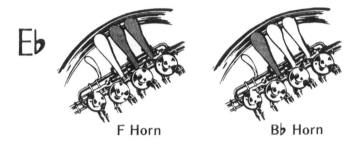

Gordon Stout wrote this solo especially for this book. He started composing at a very early age and eventually attended Eastman School of Music where he earned degrees in both Performance and Composition. His works are internationally performed and have drawn favorable comments from America's own Aaron Copland. He is presently teaching percussion, theory, and composition at St. Mary's College in Maryland and continues composing and performing.

One of the unusual points of this solo is the frequent changes of meter. This is a characteristic of much of contemporary music. Whenever you are changing meters, keep one unit of beat steady in your mind. In this solo always think of a quarter note as constant. Then as the meter changes, put 2, 3, or 4 quarter notes in a measure. Practice changing meters in the following exercise.

PREPARATION 16

Measures 1-26 The piano has the long introduction, so be sure to count carefully all of your measures rest. This will be quite a challenge at first, for there are many meter changes. But after hearing the tape and watching your part, you will eventually get so you may not need to count all of the measures, but will instead learn the sound of the music before your entrance.

Measures 27-34 Beginning in measure 31 there are several measures written in the bass clef. It is customary to use leger lines for several notes below middle "C". Since there are several measures in this area, it is easier to write it in the bass clef.

When you first began playing the horn, you learned that with a treble clef at the beginning of a line, a note on a certain line or space is always the same note. This is also true of the bass clef. Study the illustrations below which show the relationship of the bass clef and treble clef.

ILLUSTRATION 6

ILLUSTRATION 7

These are the fingerings for F horn for the notes below middle "C".

ILLUSTRATION 8

To become familiar with playing the bass clef, practice the following exercise.

PREPARATION 17

Measures 35-44 This is the beginning of a very pretty melodic section that should be played with lots of expression and dynamics. Observe the special instructions such as "moving along", "slightly faster", and "rit.". The music is constantly moving forward and slowing down in a kind of nervous energy.

Measures 45-63 Listen carefully to the accelerando in the piano from measure 44 to measure 45. The horn part here is not difficult, but a big, full sound is of utmost importance. Be sure to count carefully because this is another section that changes meter. Keep the speed of the quarter note constant. Observe the gradual ritard from measure 59 to measure 64.

Measures 64-89 This section is again slower for four measures with a nice melody. The last four eighth notes in measure 66 are heavily accented, leading into the new mood at measure 68, where you have very loud bell tones. These are tones that are struck very hard, as if you were hitting a huge bell with a hammer. The attack is the important thing here. This is the style to the very end of the piece. Once again, be careful of the meter changes, they are very frequent. Just remember, the quarter note value remains constant, so it is not as difficult as it may look.

Be sure to work out the section in bass clef beginning in measure 68. Practice slowly and check all the fingerings.

Movement For Horn And Piano

fingering chart

DOUBLE HORN ADD THUMB KEY AND B♭ FINGERING